Situational Leadership for Nonprofit Organisations: Adapting Leadership Styles for Effective Team Management

Introduction

Welcome to the comprehensive guide on situational leadership specifically tailored for nonprofit organizations. This book aims to equip leaders with the knowledge and skills needed to effectively lead and manage their teams by adapting their leadership style to meet the needs of the situation and their team members. Our journey together will cover various aspects of leadership, from understanding different management styles to improving job satisfaction and team morale.

Nonprofit organizations often operate in dynamic and challenging environments. They must address diverse stakeholder needs, often with limited resources. Effective leadership in this context requires flexibility, adaptability, and a deep understanding of both management and leadership principles. This book will provide you with practical strategies, insights, and tools to enhance your leadership capabilities and drive your organization toward success.

Learning Objectives

By the end of this book, you will:

- Understand the different styles of management and leadership.
- Gain clarity on the management mix and leadership approach.
- Embed a unified language of performance throughout the business entity for setting goals and expectations.
- Comprehend the impact of over-supervision and under-supervision.
- Accurately assess the performance readiness of individuals and teams.
- Set goals for team members and align them with the organization's goals.
- Create systems to track the completion and performance of tasks.
- Understand how to set goals and evaluate performance.
- Manage the growth of individuals and teams to take on more complex assignments.
- Improve job satisfaction and the morale of the team.
- Develop a personal growth plan.

Who Should Read this Book?

This book is designed for:

- Directors and C-Level Executives.
- Senior Management Team members.
- Heads of Departments.
- General Managers.
- Strategic Planners and Business Analysts.
- Managers, Supervisors, and those involved in managing teams.
- Aspiring leaders who wish to lead and manage teams in the future.

- Individuals who understand the need for both autocratic and collaborative management styles and wish to know when each is appropriate.
- Leaders with high potential.

Chapter 1: Introduction to Situational Leadership

Leadership is not a one-size-fits-all skill. Situational leadership, developed by Paul Hersey and Ken Blanchard, is based on the idea that there is no single best way to lead a team. Instead, effective leadership depends on the situation and the development level of the team members. This approach is particularly effective in nonprofit organizations, where the dynamics and challenges can be unique and varied.

What is Situational Leadership?

Situational leadership is a flexible, adaptable approach that allows leaders to modify their style to meet the needs of their team members and the tasks at hand. By doing so, leaders can provide the right amount of direction and support, ensuring that their teams are both effective and motivated.

The Origins of Situational Leadership

The concept of situational leadership was introduced by Paul Hersey and Ken Blanchard in their book "Management of Organizational Behavior." They identified that effective leaders adjust their leadership style based on the maturity of their followers, considering their ability and willingness to perform tasks. This approach recognizes that leadership is not static and must be tailored to the context and the people involved.

Importance in Nonprofit Organizations

Nonprofits often face unique challenges, such as limited resources, diverse stakeholder needs, and varying levels of team experience. A situational leadership approach allows leaders to adapt to these challenges by providing the right amount of direction and support to their team members. This flexibility is crucial for navigating the often unpredictable and resource-constrained environment of nonprofit organizations.

Case Study: Adaptive Leadership in Action

Consider a nonprofit organization focused on community health initiatives. The team consists of medical professionals, community workers, and volunteers. Each group has different levels of expertise and motivation. The leader must adapt their style when dealing with each group. For medical professionals, a delegating style may be appropriate, allowing them autonomy to make decisions. For volunteers, a more directing style may be needed to provide clear instructions and guidance.

Practical Exercise: Reflecting on Leadership Styles

1. Think of a recent project where you led a diverse team.
2. Identify the different levels of experience and motivation within your team.
3. Reflect on how you adjusted your leadership style to meet the needs of different team members.
4. Consider how you could further adapt your approach in future projects.

Understanding Leadership Styles in Depth

Situational leadership is more than just adapting to the situation; it involves understanding the core principles behind each leadership style and when to use them. Let's explore these styles in more depth:

- **Directing (High Directive, Low Supportive)**: This style involves providing clear instructions and closely supervising tasks. It's most effective when team members are new or inexperienced and need explicit guidance to understand their roles and responsibilities.
- **Coaching (High Directive, High Supportive)**: This style combines directive behavior with supportive behavior. It is effective when team members need both guidance and encouragement. Leaders provide direction but also seek input and encourage team members.
- **Supporting (Low Directive, High Supportive)**: Here, leaders provide less direction and more support. This style is suitable for team members who have the competence but may lack confidence or motivation. The leader's role is to facilitate, listen, and provide support to boost morale.
- **Delegating (Low Directive, Low Supportive)**: This style is used when team members are competent and motivated. Leaders can delegate tasks with minimal supervision, trusting team members to carry out their responsibilities independently.

Applying Situational Leadership in Nonprofit Organizations

In nonprofit organizations, the application of situational leadership can be particularly challenging due to the diverse range of activities and team members. Leaders must be adept at assessing the competence and commitment of their team members and choosing the appropriate leadership style. This can involve:

- Conducting regular assessments of team member performance and development.
- Providing ongoing training and development opportunities to enhance skills and confidence.
- Creating a culture of open communication where team members feel comfortable sharing their needs and feedback.
- Recognizing and rewarding achievements to maintain high levels of motivation and commitment.

Advanced Strategies in Situational Leadership

To further enhance the effectiveness of situational leadership, consider integrating the following advanced strategies:

- **Emotional Intelligence (EI)**: Develop your emotional intelligence to better understand and manage your own emotions and those of your team members. High EI enables leaders to build stronger relationships and create a positive work environment.
- **Adaptive Leadership**: Beyond just situational leadership, adaptive leadership involves navigating complex and changing environments by encouraging experimentation, learning from failures, and adjusting strategies accordingly.
- **Resilience Building**: Foster resilience within your team to help them cope with challenges and setbacks. Resilient teams are better equipped to maintain performance and morale in the face of adversity.

Example: Using Emotional Intelligence in Leadership

A nonprofit leader with high emotional intelligence might recognize when a team member is feeling overwhelmed and offer support or adjust their workload. This not only helps the team member manage stress but also strengthens the leader-team member relationship.

Example: Implementing Adaptive Leadership

A nonprofit organization facing funding cuts might use adaptive leadership by exploring alternative revenue streams, encouraging innovative solutions from team members, and remaining flexible in their strategic planning.

Example: Building Resilience in a Team

A nonprofit leader can build resilience in their team by providing training on stress management techniques, promoting a supportive work environment, and encouraging open communication about challenges and coping strategies.

Chapter 2: Understanding Management and Leadership Styles

Management and leadership are often used interchangeably, but they are distinct concepts. Management involves planning, organizing, and coordinating resources, while leadership is about inspiring and motivating people. An effective leader needs to be both a good manager and a good leader.

Management Styles

There are three primary management styles:

1. **Autocratic**: The manager makes decisions unilaterally. This style is efficient in urgent situations but may stifle creativity and innovation. It's useful in crisis situations where quick decision-making is critical.
2. **Democratic**: The manager involves team members in decision-making. This style encourages team input and fosters collaboration but can be time-consuming. It is effective in situations where diverse perspectives are valuable and time permits.
3. **Laissez-faire**: The manager provides little guidance and allows team members to make decisions. This style fosters innovation and autonomy but may lead to a lack of direction. It works well when team members are highly skilled and motivated.

Example: Autocratic Management Style

Imagine a nonprofit focused on disaster relief. During an emergency, the director must make quick decisions about resource allocation and volunteer deployment. An autocratic style is necessary to ensure timely and decisive action, although it may limit input from team members.

Example: Democratic Management Style

A nonprofit organization dedicated to community development might involve its team in decision-making processes for new projects. By gathering diverse perspectives, the organization can develop more comprehensive and effective strategies, though it might take longer to reach consensus.

Example: Laissez-faire Management Style

A nonprofit promoting creative arts may benefit from a laissez-faire approach, allowing artists and creative professionals to have the freedom to innovate and express themselves. However, this style requires a clear understanding of overall goals to avoid misalignment.

Leadership Styles

Situational leadership, as proposed by Hersey and Blanchard, includes:

- **Directing**: High directive, low supportive behavior. This style is useful when team members are new or inexperienced.
- **Coaching**: High directive, high supportive behavior. This style is effective when team members need guidance but are motivated.
- **Supporting**: Low directive, high supportive behavior. This style is suitable for experienced team members who need support rather than direction.
- **Delegating**: Low directive, low supportive behavior. This style is best for highly competent and motivated team members who can work independently.

Case Study: Applying Leadership Styles

Imagine you are leading a team at a nonprofit organization focused on educational outreach. Your team includes new interns, experienced educators, and administrative staff. For the new interns, a directing style is needed to provide clear instructions and supervision. For the experienced educators, a supporting style helps them feel valued and supported while they use their expertise. For the administrative staff, a delegating style allows them to manage their tasks independently, reflecting their competence and commitment.

Practical Exercise: Identifying Your Leadership Style

1. Reflect on your leadership experiences.
2. Identify situations where you used each of the four leadership styles.
3. Analyze the outcomes of using these styles.
4. Consider how you can adapt your style in future situations to better meet the needs of your team.

Integrating Management and Leadership

Effective leaders integrate management and leadership skills to create a balanced approach. This integration involves:

- **Strategic Planning**: Developing long-term goals and strategies to achieve the organization's mission.
- **Operational Management**: Ensuring that day-to-day activities align with strategic objectives.
- **People Management**: Inspiring, motivating, and developing team members to reach their full potential.
- **Resource Management**: Allocating resources efficiently to support both short-term and long-term goals.

By combining these elements, leaders can create a cohesive and effective team that is capable of achieving the organization's objectives.

Advanced Concepts in Management and Leadership

To further refine your approach, consider incorporating advanced concepts:

- **Transformational Leadership**: Focus on inspiring and motivating team members to exceed expectations and achieve their full potential. Transformational leaders create a vision for the future and encourage innovation.
- **Servant Leadership**: Prioritize the needs of your team members and empower them to perform at their best. Servant leaders build strong relationships and create a supportive work environment.
- **Transactional Leadership**: Use rewards and punishments to manage performance and achieve specific goals. This style can be effective in situations where clear expectations and accountability are needed.

Example: Transformational Leadership

A nonprofit leader using transformational leadership might inspire their team by sharing a compelling vision for the organization's future, encouraging creative solutions to challenges, and recognizing and celebrating achievements.

Example: Servant Leadership

A nonprofit leader practicing servant leadership might focus on supporting their team by providing the resources and training needed to succeed, actively listening to their concerns, and fostering a collaborative and inclusive work environment.

Example: Transactional Leadership

A nonprofit leader using transactional leadership might set clear performance goals for fundraising efforts and offer incentives for reaching targets while addressing underperformance with specific corrective actions.

Chapter 3: The Management Mix and Leadership Approach

The management mix involves balancing various management styles and leadership approaches to achieve the best outcomes. It's about knowing when to be directive and when to be supportive.

Assessing the Situation

To effectively manage a team, leaders need to understand the strengths and weaknesses of each approach and apply them based on the specific needs of their team members and the tasks at hand. Start by assessing the situation. Consider factors such as the complexity of the task, the experience and competence of the team members, and the urgency of the situation.

Determining the Appropriate Approach

- **Complexity of the Task**: More complex tasks may require a more directive approach to ensure clarity and precision.
- **Experience of Team Members**: Experienced team members may benefit from a supportive or delegating approach, while less experienced members may need more direction.
- **Urgency of the Situation**: Urgent situations may necessitate an autocratic or directive approach to make quick decisions and actions.

Example: Task Complexity

A nonprofit organization working on a complex environmental conservation project may require detailed planning and directive leadership to ensure all aspects are addressed. However, for routine tasks like monthly reporting, a more laissez-faire approach may be sufficient.

Example: Team Experience

A team of seasoned professionals working on a strategic plan for a nonprofit can be given more autonomy (delegating style), while new hires working on their first project may need more hands-on guidance (directing style).

Case Study: Implementing a New Program

Imagine you're leading a team to implement a new community outreach program. The team includes both experienced staff and new volunteers. You might start with a coaching style, providing clear direction and support, and gradually shift to a supporting style as the team gains confidence and experience. By assessing the situation and adapting your approach, you can ensure that your team receives the appropriate level of guidance and support.

Practical Tips for Balancing the Management Mix

- **Communicate Clearly**: Ensure that your team understands their roles, responsibilities, and the overall goals of the project.
- **Provide Feedback**: Regular feedback helps team members understand how they are performing and where they can improve.
- **Be Flexible**: Be willing to adjust your leadership style based on the evolving needs of your team and the situation.
- **Encourage Collaboration**: Foster an environment where team members feel comfortable sharing ideas and collaborating.

Practical Exercise: Assessing Your Management Mix

1. Identify a recent project or task you managed.
2. Analyze the leadership style you used for each team member.
3. Reflect on the outcomes and consider whether a different style might have been more effective.
4. Plan how you can apply these insights to future projects.

Advanced Techniques for Balancing the Management Mix

To further refine your approach, consider using advanced techniques for balancing the management mix:

- **Leadership Flexibility**: Continuously develop your ability to switch between different leadership styles as needed. Practice self-awareness and adaptability to respond effectively to changing circumstances.
- **Team Development**: Invest in the ongoing development of your team members. Provide opportunities for skill-building, mentorship, and cross-training to enhance their capabilities and readiness for various tasks.
- **Conflict Resolution**: Develop strong conflict resolution skills to manage disagreements and tensions within the team. Effective conflict resolution helps maintain a positive and productive work environment.

Example: Leadership Flexibility

A nonprofit leader might practice leadership flexibility by adapting their style based on individual team members' needs and the specific demands of each project. This approach ensures that team members receive the right level of support and direction.

Example: Team Development

A nonprofit organization might offer regular training sessions, workshops, and mentorship programs to support the professional growth of their staff. This investment in development helps build a more capable and resilient team.

Example: Conflict Resolution

A nonprofit leader might use conflict resolution techniques, such as mediation and active listening, to address disputes within the team. By facilitating open and respectful communication, the leader can help resolve conflicts and strengthen team cohesion.

Chapter 4: Setting Goals and Expectations

Setting clear goals and expectations is crucial for providing direction and motivation. It ensures that everyone is aligned and working towards the same objectives.

Importance of Goal Setting

When team members understand what is expected of them and how their work contributes to the organization's goals, they are more likely to be engaged and productive. One effective method for setting goals is the SMART framework.

SMART Goals

SMART stands for:

- **Specific**: Clearly define what needs to be achieved.
- **Measurable**: Ensure the goal can be tracked and measured.
- **Achievable**: Set realistic goals that are attainable.
- **Relevant**: Align the goal with broader organizational objectives.
- **Time-bound**: Set a deadline for achieving the goal.

Example: Creating SMART Goals

- **Specific**: Clearly define the goal. Instead of "Increase community engagement," specify "Increase community engagement by 20% through targeted outreach programs."
- **Measurable**: Determine how you will measure progress. For example, track the number of new community members engaged.
- **Achievable**: Ensure the goal is realistic given your resources and constraints. Consider if a 20% increase is attainable within your timeframe.
- **Relevant**: Align the goal with your organization's mission. Ensure it contributes to your overall objectives.
- **Time-bound**: Set a deadline for achieving the goal. For example, "Increase community engagement by 20% within six months."

Case Study: Setting SMART Goals for a Nonprofit

A nonprofit organization focused on reducing homelessness might set the following SMART goal: "Reduce the number of homeless individuals in our city by 15% within the next year through expanded outreach and support services." This goal is specific, measurable, achievable, relevant, and time-bound, providing clear direction and motivation for the team.

Aligning Goals

Aligning individual goals with the organization's objectives ensures that everyone is working towards the same mission and vision. When setting goals, involve your team members in the process. This not only ensures buy-in but also provides valuable insights and fosters a sense of ownership.

Communicating Goals

Clear communication is key to setting expectations. Make sure your team understands the goals, the steps needed to achieve them, and the criteria for success. Regular check-ins and progress reviews help keep everyone on track and provide opportunities to address any challenges that arise.

Tracking Progress

Use tools and systems to track progress towards goals. This could be project management software, progress reports, or regular team meetings. By setting clear goals and expectations, you provide your team with the direction and motivation they need to succeed.

Example: Using Project Management Software

A nonprofit organization might use tools like Asana or Trello to set and track goals. Each task can be assigned to a team member with deadlines and progress updates. This ensures everyone is aware of their responsibilities and can see the progress being made towards the overall goal.

Example: Regular Progress Reports

Monthly progress reports can be used to document achievements, identify challenges, and adjust strategies as needed. This keeps the team informed and engaged, ensuring that everyone is aligned with the organization's goals.

Practical Tips for Effective Goal Setting

- **Involve the Team**: Encourage team members to participate in goal setting to ensure their commitment and engagement.
- **Break Down Goals**: Divide larger goals into smaller, manageable tasks with clear milestones.
- **Use Visual Aids**: Utilize charts, graphs, and progress trackers to visually represent progress.
- **Celebrate Milestones**: Recognize and celebrate when milestones are achieved to maintain motivation.

Practical Exercise: Setting and Achieving Goals

1. Identify a goal you want to achieve with your team.
2. Apply the SMART criteria to refine the goal.
3. Develop a plan to achieve the goal, including milestones and deadlines.
4. Communicate the goal and plan to your team.
5. Track progress and adjust the plan as needed.

Advanced Goal Setting Techniques

In addition to the SMART framework, there are other advanced goal-setting techniques that can help enhance your goal-setting process:

- **OKRs (Objectives and Key Results)**: This method involves setting ambitious objectives and defining measurable key results to track progress. OKRs can align individual and team goals with the organization's strategic objectives.
- **Backward Goal Setting**: Start with the end goal in mind and work backward to identify the steps needed to achieve it. This method ensures that each step is aligned with the ultimate objective.
- **Cascading Goals**: Align goals across all levels of the organization. This method ensures that individual goals support team goals, which in turn support organizational goals.

Example: Implementing OKRs

A nonprofit organization focused on environmental conservation might set an OKR like this:

- **Objective**: Improve community engagement in conservation efforts.
- **Key Results**:
    o Organize five community events within the next six months.
    o Increase volunteer participation by 30%.
    o Partner with three local schools for educational programs.

Example: Backward Goal Setting

A nonprofit planning a major fundraising event might use backward goal setting:

- **End Goal**: Raise $100,000 at the annual gala.
- **Steps**:
    o Secure venue and date (3 months prior).

- o Develop marketing plan and materials (2 months prior).
- o Reach out to potential sponsors and donors (1 month prior).
- o Finalize event logistics and volunteer assignments (2 weeks prior).

Example: Cascading Goals

An education-focused nonprofit might set cascading goals:

- **Organizational Goal**: Improve literacy rates by 20% within three years.
- **Team Goal**: Develop and implement new literacy programs.
- **Individual Goal**: Train five new literacy volunteers each quarter.

Goal Setting Frameworks

In addition to SMART and OKRs, consider exploring other goal-setting frameworks:

- **BHAG (Big Hairy Audacious Goals)**: These are long-term, ambitious goals that can inspire and motivate your team. BHAGs are designed to challenge the organization and push it towards extraordinary achievements.
- **HARD Goals**: This framework focuses on goals that are Heartfelt, Animated, Required, and Difficult. It emphasizes the emotional and motivational aspects of goal setting.
- **V2MOM (Vision, Values, Methods, Obstacles, and Measures)**: Created by Marc Benioff, this framework helps align goals with the organization's vision and

values while identifying methods, obstacles, and measures for success.

Example: Setting a BHAG

A nonprofit organization dedicated to eradicating hunger might set a BHAG to "End hunger in our community within the next decade by implementing sustainable food programs and advocacy initiatives."

Example: Applying the HARD Goals Framework

A nonprofit focused on youth development might set a HARD goal like this:

- **Heartfelt**: "Empower 500 underserved youth with leadership skills."
- **Animated**: "Create a vibrant and engaging leadership camp."
- **Required**: "Secure funding and resources to launch the program."
- **Difficult**: "Achieve a 95% program completion rate."

Example: Using V2MOM

A nonprofit organization might use the V2MOM framework to align a new initiative:

- **Vision**: "Increase access to clean water in rural areas."
- **Values**: "Sustainability, Community Empowerment, and Health."
- **Methods**: "Partner with local organizations, implement water filtration systems, and provide education on hygiene."

- **Obstacles**: "Limited funding, logistical challenges, and community resistance."
- **Measures**: "Track the number of households with clean water access, monitor health outcomes, and evaluate community engagement."

Chapter 5: Over-Supervision vs. Under-Supervision

Over-supervision occurs when a leader provides too much direction and control, which can stifle creativity and independence. Under-supervision, on the other hand, happens when a leader provides too little guidance, leading to confusion and lack of direction. Both over-supervision and under-supervision can negatively impact team performance and morale. Finding the right balance is crucial for effective leadership.

Impact of Over-Supervision

Over-supervision can:

- Reduce team members' sense of ownership and responsibility.
- Stifle creativity and innovation.
- Lead to dependency on the leader for decision-making.
- Cause frustration and low morale.

When team members feel micromanaged, they may become disengaged and less motivated to contribute their best efforts.

Case Study: The Pitfalls of Over-Supervision

Consider a nonprofit organization where the leader is heavily involved in every decision, down to the smallest detail. While the leader's intentions may be good, team members feel they have no autonomy, and their ideas are not valued. This leads to high turnover as team members seek environments where they can have more control over their work.

Example: Over-Supervision in a Fundraising Campaign

A nonprofit leader overseeing a fundraising campaign might insist on approving every communication and strategy. This level of control can slow down the process and prevent team members from using their creativity and expertise. The result is a less effective campaign and a demotivated team.

Impact of Under-Supervision

Under-supervision can:

- Lead to confusion and lack of direction.
- Result in inconsistent performance and quality of work.
- Cause team members to feel unsupported.
- Increase the risk of mistakes and missed deadlines.

When team members do not receive enough guidance, they may struggle to understand their roles and responsibilities, leading to decreased productivity and job satisfaction.

Case Study: The Dangers of Under-Supervision

In another nonprofit, the leader takes a hands-off approach, assuming that team members will figure things out on their own. However, without adequate guidance, projects often go off track, deadlines are missed, and team members feel overwhelmed and unsupported.

Example: Under-Supervision in Program Development

A nonprofit organization developing a new program may leave the team to manage the project independently without clear guidance or support. This can lead to misunderstandings, missed deadlines, and a program that does not meet the organization's standards or goals.

Finding the Right Balance

To find the right balance, consider:

- **The complexity of the task**: More complex tasks may require more direction.
- **The experience and competence of the team members**: Experienced team members may benefit from a supportive or delegating approach.
- **The level of support needed**: Provide the necessary support to achieve the desired outcomes.

Practical Tips for Balancing Supervision

- **Set Clear Expectations**: Ensure that team members understand their roles, responsibilities, and the overall goals of the project.
- **Monitor Progress**: Regularly check in on progress and provide feedback to keep team members on track.
- **Encourage Independence**: Allow team members to take ownership of their tasks and make decisions within their scope.

- **Be Available for Support**: Make it clear that you are available for guidance and support when needed.

Example: Balancing Supervision in a Community Project

A nonprofit leader managing a community project might set clear expectations and provide initial guidance to new volunteers. As volunteers become more familiar with their roles, the leader can gradually reduce supervision, allowing them more autonomy while remaining available for support.

Practical Exercise: Assessing Supervision Levels

1. Reflect on a recent project where you provided supervision.
2. Analyze whether your level of supervision was appropriate for each team member.
3. Identify any instances of over-supervision or under-supervision.
4. Develop a plan to adjust your supervision levels for future projects.

Advanced Supervision Techniques

To further refine your approach to supervision, consider incorporating advanced techniques:

- **Situational Awareness**: Continuously assess the situation and adjust your supervision style as needed. Be aware of changes in the task complexity, team dynamics, and individual performance.
- **Feedback Loops**: Establish regular feedback loops where team members can share their experiences and provide input on the level of supervision they need.

This promotes a collaborative approach to supervision.

- **Empowerment Strategies**: Focus on empowering team members by providing the resources and training they need to succeed. Empowerment reduces the need for constant supervision and builds a sense of ownership.

Example: Implementing Situational Awareness

A nonprofit leader might conduct regular check-ins with team members to assess their progress and needs. If a team member is struggling with a new task, the leader can temporarily increase supervision and support until the team member feels more confident.

Example: Establishing Feedback Loops

A nonprofit organization might hold monthly team meetings where members can discuss their experiences and provide feedback on the level of supervision they receive. This feedback helps the leader adjust their approach to better meet the team's needs.

Example: Empowerment Strategies

A nonprofit leader might provide training sessions on project management tools to empower team members to manage their tasks independently. By equipping team members with the necessary skills, the leader can reduce the need for constant supervision.

Supervisory Styles and Techniques

Explore different supervisory styles and techniques to find what works best for your team:

- **Directive Supervision**: Provide clear instructions and closely monitor progress. This style is effective for new or inexperienced team members who need explicit guidance.
- **Participative Supervision**: Involve team members in decision-making and problem-solving. This approach encourages collaboration and ownership.
- **Supportive Supervision**: Focus on providing emotional and motivational support. This style is beneficial for team members who need encouragement and recognition.
- **Delegative Supervision**: Delegate tasks and responsibilities to capable team members. This style fosters autonomy and professional growth.

Example: Applying Directive Supervision

A nonprofit leader might use directive supervision for a new team member learning the organization's policies and procedures. By providing step-by-step instructions and close monitoring, the leader ensures the team member understands their role.

Example: Using Participative Supervision

A nonprofit leader might use participative supervision during a strategic planning session, encouraging team members to contribute their ideas and insights. This approach leverages the collective expertise of the team.

Example: Implementing Supportive Supervision

A nonprofit leader might use supportive supervision for a team member facing personal challenges. By offering empathy, encouragement, and flexibility, the leader helps the team member maintain productivity and morale.

Example: Utilizing Delegative Supervision

A nonprofit leader might use delegative supervision for a seasoned project manager, entrusting them with the responsibility to lead a new initiative. This approach empowers the project manager and demonstrates trust in their abilities.

Chapter 6: Assessing Performance Readiness

Performance readiness refers to the ability and willingness of team members to perform a task. It includes their competence and commitment to the task. Assessing performance readiness helps leaders tailor their approach to meet the needs of their team members, providing the right amount of direction and support.

Competence and Commitment

- **Competence**: The skills and knowledge needed to perform a task.
- **Commitment**: The motivation and confidence to complete the task.

Both competence and commitment are crucial for performance readiness. A team member may have high competence but low commitment, or vice versa. Understanding these factors helps leaders provide the appropriate support.

Assessing Competence

To assess competence, consider:

- **Previous Experience and Skills**: Review the team member's past performance and relevant skills.
- **Training and Development Needs**: Identify any gaps in knowledge or skills that may need to be addressed.
- **Performance in Similar Tasks**: Evaluate how the team member has performed on similar tasks in the past.

Ask yourself: Does the team member have the necessary skills and knowledge to perform the task? If not, what training or support do they need?

Example: Assessing Competence in a Grant Writing Team

A nonprofit leader might assess the competence of a grant writing team by reviewing their previous grant applications, identifying areas where additional training or support is needed, and providing opportunities for professional development.

Assessing Commitment

To assess commitment, consider:

- **Motivation and Enthusiasm**: Observe the team member's level of interest and enthusiasm for the task.

- **Confidence in Their Ability**: Assess whether the team member feels confident in their ability to complete the task.
- **Willingness to Take on Responsibility**: Evaluate the team member's willingness to take ownership of the task.

Ask yourself: Is the team member motivated and confident? If not, how can you increase their commitment and confidence?

Example: Assessing Commitment in a Volunteer Coordinator

A nonprofit leader might assess the commitment of a volunteer coordinator by observing their enthusiasm for organizing volunteer activities, their confidence in managing volunteers, and their willingness to take on additional responsibilities.

Development Levels

Based on their competence and commitment, team members can be classified into four development levels:

- **D1: Low competence, high commitment**. These team members are enthusiastic but lack the skills and experience.
- **D2: Some competence, low commitment**. These team members have some skills but may lack confidence or motivation.
- **D3: Moderate to high competence, variable commitment**. These team members are skilled but may be inconsistent in their motivation.
- **D4: High competence, high commitment**. These team members are skilled and motivated.

Each development level requires a different leadership approach. For example, D1 team members need clear direction and close supervision, while D4 team members benefit from delegation and autonomy.

Practical Tips for Assessing Performance Readiness

- **Conduct Regular Assessments**: Regularly evaluate the competence and commitment of your team members.
- **Provide Training and Development**: Address any gaps in skills or knowledge through training and development opportunities.
- **Foster a Motivating Environment**: Create an environment that encourages motivation and confidence.
- **Adjust Your Approach**: Tailor your leadership style to match the development level of your team members.

Example: Tailoring Leadership Approaches

A nonprofit leader might provide detailed instructions and close supervision to a new team member (D1) working on their first project. For a highly experienced and motivated team member (D4), the leader might delegate tasks and provide minimal supervision, allowing the team member to work independently.

Practical Exercise: Assessing Performance Readiness

1. Identify a task or project your team is working on.

2. Assess the competence and commitment of each team member involved.
3. Classify each team member into one of the four development levels.
4. Develop a plan to provide the appropriate level of direction and support for each team member.

Advanced Assessment Techniques

To further refine your assessment of performance readiness, consider using advanced techniques:

- **360-Degree Feedback**: Gather feedback from multiple sources, including peers, subordinates, and supervisors, to gain a comprehensive view of a team member's performance.
- **Self-Assessment**: Encourage team members to assess their own competence and commitment. This self-reflection can provide valuable insights and promote personal growth.
- **Behavioral Assessments**: Use behavioral assessments, such as the DISC profile, to understand team members' natural tendencies and preferences. This information can help tailor your leadership approach.

Example: Implementing 360-Degree Feedback

A nonprofit leader might implement a 360-degree feedback system where team members provide feedback on each other's performance. This feedback is then used to identify strengths and areas for improvement.

Example: Encouraging Self-Assessment

A nonprofit organization might provide self-assessment tools for team members to evaluate their own competence and commitment. These tools can include questionnaires or reflective exercises.

Example: Using Behavioral Assessments

A nonprofit leader might use the DISC profile to understand the behavioral styles of team members. For example, a team member with a high "D" (Dominance) profile might prefer direct communication and autonomy, while a team member with a high "S" (Steadiness) profile might prefer supportive and collaborative environments.

Creating a Performance Readiness Plan

Develop a comprehensive performance readiness plan that includes:

- **Initial Assessments**: Conduct initial assessments of competence and commitment for all team members.
- **Regular Check-Ins**: Schedule regular check-ins to reassess performance readiness and adjust support as needed.
- **Development Opportunities**: Identify and provide training and development opportunities to enhance skills and confidence.
- **Feedback Mechanisms**: Establish feedback mechanisms to continuously gather insights from team members and adjust your approach.

Example: Performance Readiness Plan for a New Initiative

A nonprofit leader might develop a performance readiness plan for a new initiative that includes initial assessments of team members' skills and motivation, regular progress reviews, targeted training sessions, and opportunities for team members to provide feedback on their needs and experiences.

Chapter 7: Tracking Performance and Growth

Tracking performance is crucial for understanding progress, identifying areas for improvement, and ensuring that goals are being met. It provides a basis for feedback and development. Effective performance tracking helps leaders support their team's growth and ensures that tasks are completed to a high standard.

Performance Tracking Systems

There are various tools and systems you can use to track performance, such as:

- **Project Management Software**: Tools like Asana, Trello, or Monday.com can help you organize tasks, set deadlines, and track progress.
- **Performance Dashboards**: Visual dashboards can provide an overview of key performance indicators (KPIs) and metrics.
- **Regular Progress Reports**: Written reports can document progress, challenges, and next steps.
- **Team Meetings and Check-Ins**: Regular meetings provide an opportunity to discuss progress, address issues, and plan next steps.

Choose the tools that best fit your team's needs and ensure they are used consistently.

Example: Using Project Management Software

A nonprofit organization might use Asana to track the progress of a new community program. Each task is assigned to a team member with specific deadlines and progress updates. This ensures that everyone is aware of their responsibilities and the overall progress of the project.

Example: Performance Dashboards

A nonprofit might use a performance dashboard to monitor key metrics, such as the number of clients served, funds raised, and program outcomes. This provides a visual representation of progress and helps identify areas that need attention.

Setting Milestones

Set clear milestones for each task or project. Milestones are specific points in the project timeline that mark significant progress. They help keep the team focused and motivated.

For example, if you're running a community outreach program, milestones could include:

- Completing the planning phase.
- Launching the program.
- Achieving certain participation targets.

Example: Milestones in a Fundraising Campaign

A nonprofit organization might set milestones for a fundraising campaign, such as securing the first major donor, reaching 50% of the fundraising goal, and holding a major fundraising event. These milestones help keep the team focused and motivated.

Providing Feedback

Regular feedback is essential for performance improvement. Provide constructive feedback that highlights strengths and areas for development. Use specific examples and be clear about your expectations. Feedback should be timely and relevant. Regular check-ins and performance reviews provide opportunities for ongoing feedback and support.

Example: Providing Feedback in a Volunteer Program

A nonprofit leader might provide feedback to volunteers by acknowledging their contributions and suggesting ways to improve. For example, "You did a great job engaging with participants at the event. Next time, try to focus on providing more detailed information about our programs."

Supporting Growth

Support your team's growth by identifying development needs and providing opportunities for learning and development. This could include training, mentoring, and stretch assignments. Encourage your team members to take on new challenges and develop their skills. This not only helps them grow but also strengthens the overall capability of the team.

Example: Supporting Growth Through Training

A nonprofit leader might identify a need for grant writing skills within the team and arrange for training sessions. This not only enhances the team's capabilities but also increases their confidence and job satisfaction.

Recognizing Achievement

Recognize and celebrate achievements. Acknowledging your team's hard work and successes boosts morale and motivation. Recognition can be formal, such as awards or promotions, or informal, such as verbal praise and thank-you notes. Make recognition a regular part of your leadership practice.

Example: Recognizing Achievement in a Program Manager

A nonprofit leader might recognize a program manager's achievement by presenting an award at a team meeting and sharing the success story in the organization's newsletter. This public acknowledgment boosts the program manager's morale and motivates the entire team.

Continuous Improvement

Foster a culture of continuous improvement. Encourage your team to reflect on their performance, identify areas for improvement, and set new goals. Continuous improvement ensures that your team is always learning, growing, and striving for excellence. By effectively tracking performance and supporting your team's growth, you can create a high-performing, motivated team.

Example: Continuous Improvement in a Health Initiative

A nonprofit organization running a health initiative might hold regular review meetings to assess program outcomes, gather feedback from participants, and identify areas for improvement. This process ensures that the program remains effective and responsive to community needs.

Practical Tips for Tracking Performance and Growth

- **Use Visual Aids**: Utilize charts, graphs, and dashboards to visually represent progress.
- **Set Clear Expectations**: Ensure that team members understand what is expected of them and how their performance will be measured.
- **Encourage Self-Assessment**: Encourage team members to assess their own performance and identify areas for improvement.
- **Provide Regular Updates**: Keep team members informed about progress and any changes to plans or goals.

Practical Exercise: Tracking Performance

1. Choose a project or task your team is currently working on.
2. Identify the key performance indicators (KPIs) you will use to track progress.
3. Set clear milestones and deadlines for the project.
4. Develop a plan for providing regular feedback and support.
5. Use the chosen performance tracking tools to monitor progress.

Advanced Performance Tracking Techniques

To enhance your performance tracking process, consider using advanced techniques:

- **Balanced Scorecard**: This method tracks performance across multiple dimensions, such as financial, customer, internal processes, and learning and growth. It provides a comprehensive view of organizational performance.
- **Key Performance Indicators (KPIs)**: Identify specific, measurable indicators that align with your strategic goals. Regularly review and update KPIs to ensure they remain relevant.
- **Benchmarking**: Compare your organization's performance with similar organizations or industry standards to identify areas for improvement.

Example: Implementing a Balanced Scorecard

A nonprofit organization might implement a balanced scorecard to track performance across various dimensions:

- **Financial**: Track fundraising revenue and expense ratios.
- **Customer**: Measure client satisfaction and service delivery.
- **Internal Processes**: Monitor program efficiency and effectiveness.
- **Learning and Growth**: Assess staff training and development initiatives.

Example: Identifying Key Performance Indicators

A nonprofit focused on education might identify the following KPIs:

- **Student Enrollment**: Track the number of students enrolled in programs.
- **Graduation Rates**: Measure the percentage of students who complete the program.
- **Volunteer Hours**: Monitor the total hours contributed by volunteers.

Example: Benchmarking Performance

A nonprofit organization might benchmark its fundraising performance against similar organizations. This comparison helps identify best practices and areas for improvement.

Enhancing Performance Reviews

Enhance your performance reviews to ensure they are effective and meaningful:

- **Prepare Thoroughly**: Gather relevant data, feedback, and performance metrics before the review.
- **Create a Positive Environment**: Conduct reviews in a supportive and non-threatening environment to encourage open dialogue.
- **Focus on Development**: Emphasize growth and development opportunities rather than just evaluating past performance.
- **Set Clear Goals**: Collaboratively set clear and achievable goals for the future.

Example: Conducting Effective Performance Reviews

A nonprofit leader might conduct performance reviews by starting with positive feedback, discussing areas for improvement, and jointly setting goals for the next review period. This approach ensures that team members feel valued and motivated.

Utilizing Technology in Performance Tracking

Leverage technology to streamline and enhance your performance tracking process:

- **Automated Reporting**: Use software tools to automate the generation of performance reports, saving time and reducing errors.
- **Real-Time Data**: Utilize tools that provide real-time data and insights, allowing for timely interventions and adjustments.
- **Collaboration Platforms**: Implement collaboration platforms that facilitate communication and data sharing among team members.

Example: Using Automated Reporting Tools

A nonprofit organization might use automated reporting tools to generate weekly performance reports, providing leadership with up-to-date information on project progress and team performance.

Example: Leveraging Real-Time Data

A nonprofit leader might use real-time data dashboards to monitor the progress of a fundraising campaign, enabling them to make immediate adjustments to strategies and tactics.

Example: Implementing Collaboration Platforms

A nonprofit organization might implement a collaboration platform like Slack or Microsoft Teams to enhance communication and data sharing among team members, improving overall efficiency and coordination.

Chapter 8: Improving Job Satisfaction and Team Morale

Job satisfaction is crucial for retaining talent, improving performance, and fostering a positive work environment. When team members are satisfied with their jobs, they are more engaged, motivated, and productive. High morale leads to a cohesive, collaborative team that is better equipped to achieve its goals and overcome challenges.

Factors Influencing Job Satisfaction

Several factors influence job satisfaction, including:

- **Work-Life Balance**: Ensuring that team members have a healthy balance between work and personal life.
- **Recognition and Rewards**: Acknowledging and rewarding team members for their hard work and achievements.
- **Opportunities for Growth and Development**: Providing opportunities for professional growth and development.
- **Supportive Leadership**: Demonstrating supportive and empathetic leadership.
- **Positive Work Culture**: Fostering a positive and inclusive work environment.

As a leader, you play a crucial role in shaping these factors and creating an environment where your team can thrive.

Enhancing Work-Life Balance

Promote work-life balance by:

- **Encouraging Flexible Work Arrangements**: Offer options such as remote work, flexible hours, or compressed workweeks.
- **Respecting Personal Time and Boundaries**: Avoid contacting team members outside of work hours and encourage them to take breaks and vacations.
- **Providing Resources for Stress Management and Well-Being**: Offer resources such as wellness programs, counseling services, and stress management workshops.

Example: Enhancing Work-Life Balance in a Nonprofit

A nonprofit organization might offer flexible work hours to accommodate the diverse needs of its staff, including those with caregiving responsibilities. This flexibility helps prevent burnout and ensures that team members are energized and focused.

Recognition and Rewards

Implement a recognition and rewards program to acknowledge hard work and achievements. This can include:

- **Formal Awards and Incentives**: Offer awards, bonuses, or other incentives for outstanding performance.
- **Informal Recognition**: Provide verbal praise, thank-you notes, or public acknowledgment in meetings.

- **Opportunities for Career Advancement**: Offer promotions, new responsibilities, or professional development opportunities.

Example: Recognition in a Volunteer Program

A nonprofit leader might recognize a volunteer's exceptional contribution by presenting a certificate of appreciation at a public event and sharing their story on the organization's social media channels. This recognition boosts the volunteer's morale and encourages others to contribute.

Growth and Development

Provide opportunities for growth and development by:

- **Offering Training and Development Programs**: Provide access to workshops, courses, or certifications.
- **Encouraging Mentorship and Coaching**: Pair team members with mentors or coaches to support their development.
- **Assigning Challenging Projects**: Give team members opportunities to take on new challenges and develop new skills.

Example: Growth and Development in a Youth Program

A nonprofit organization running a youth program might offer training sessions on leadership skills for its staff and volunteers. This enhances their ability to mentor and support young people while also contributing to their professional growth.

Supportive Leadership

Demonstrate supportive leadership by:

- **Being Approachable and Available**: Make yourself accessible to your team and encourage open communication.
- **Providing Regular Feedback and Guidance**: Offer constructive feedback and support to help team members improve and grow.
- **Showing Empathy and Understanding**: Be empathetic to your team's needs and challenges and provide support when needed.

Example: Supportive Leadership in a Crisis Situation

During a crisis, a nonprofit leader might hold regular check-ins with team members to offer support, address concerns, and provide clear guidance. This approach helps maintain morale and ensures that the team feels supported.

Building a Positive Work Culture

Foster a positive work culture by:

- **Encouraging Collaboration and Teamwork**: Promote a collaborative environment where team members work together towards common goals.
- **Promoting Open Communication and Transparency**: Encourage open and honest communication and provide transparency in decision-making.

- **Celebrating Diversity and Inclusion**: Create an inclusive environment that values and respects diversity.

Example: Building a Positive Work Culture in a Multicultural Team

A nonprofit organization with a multicultural team might celebrate cultural diversity by recognizing cultural holidays, encouraging team members to share their traditions, and promoting an inclusive environment where everyone feels valued.

Developing a Personal Growth Plan

Encourage your team members to develop personal growth plans that outline their goals and the steps they need to take to achieve them. This helps them stay focused and motivated. Personal growth plans provide a roadmap for professional development and ensure that team members are continually growing and improving.

Example: Personal Growth Plan for a Program Coordinator

A program coordinator at a nonprofit organization might develop a personal growth plan that includes goals such as completing a leadership training program, taking on additional responsibilities, and pursuing a certification in project management. This plan helps the coordinator stay focused and motivated on their professional development.

Practical Tips for Improving Job Satisfaction and Team Morale

- **Foster a Positive Environment**: Create a supportive and inclusive work environment that encourages collaboration and open communication.
- **Recognize and Reward Achievements**: Regularly acknowledge and reward team members for their hard work and contributions.
- **Provide Opportunities for Growth**: Offer training, development, and career advancement opportunities.
- **Encourage Work-Life Balance**: Promote flexible work arrangements and support team members in maintaining a healthy work-life balance.

Practical Exercise: Enhancing Job Satisfaction

1. Identify a factor that influences job satisfaction in your team (e.g., work-life balance, recognition).
2. Develop a plan to address this factor and improve job satisfaction.
3. Implement the plan and monitor its impact on team morale and performance.
4. Collect feedback from team members and make adjustments as needed.

Advanced Strategies for Improving Job Satisfaction

To further enhance job satisfaction, consider implementing advanced strategies:

- **Employee Engagement Surveys**: Conduct regular surveys to gather feedback on job satisfaction and identify areas for improvement. Use the survey results to develop targeted action plans.
- **Career Development Programs**: Offer comprehensive career development programs that include mentorship, coaching, and opportunities for

advancement. Help team members create individualized career paths.

- **Wellness Initiatives**: Implement wellness initiatives that support physical, mental, and emotional well-being. This can include fitness programs, mental health resources, and wellness challenges.

Example: Implementing Employee Engagement Surveys

A nonprofit organization might conduct annual employee engagement surveys to assess job satisfaction. The survey results can highlight areas where improvements are needed, such as communication, workload management, or professional development opportunities.

Example: Career Development Programs

A nonprofit might develop a career development program that includes regular coaching sessions, access to professional development courses, and a clear path for career advancement. This program helps team members see a future with the organization and stay motivated.

Example: Wellness Initiatives

A nonprofit organization might implement wellness initiatives such as offering yoga classes, providing access to counseling services, and organizing wellness challenges that promote healthy lifestyles. These initiatives support overall well-being and enhance job satisfaction.

Creating a Recognition and Rewards Program

Develop a comprehensive recognition and rewards program that includes:

- **Formal Recognition**: Implement formal awards and recognition ceremonies to celebrate significant achievements.
- **Informal Recognition**: Encourage a culture of informal recognition through verbal praise, thank-you notes, and peer recognition.
- **Performance-Based Rewards**: Offer performance-based rewards such as bonuses, promotions, and additional responsibilities.

Example: Formal Recognition Program

A nonprofit organization might hold an annual awards ceremony to recognize outstanding contributions from staff and volunteers. Awards could include categories such as "Employee of the Year," "Volunteer of the Year," and "Team Achievement Award."

Example: Informal Recognition Culture

A nonprofit leader might encourage a culture of informal recognition by regularly acknowledging team members' efforts during meetings, sending personalized thank-you notes, and encouraging peer-to-peer recognition.

Example: Performance-Based Rewards

A nonprofit organization might offer performance-based rewards such as financial bonuses for meeting fundraising targets, promotions for consistent high performance, and opportunities to lead new initiatives.

Conclusion

In this book, we have covered the key aspects of situational leadership and how to apply them in a nonprofit context. By understanding and adapting your leadership style, setting clear goals, providing the right level of supervision, and supporting your team's growth, you can create a high-performing, motivated team.

Effective leadership is about adapting to the needs of your team and the situation. We hope you found this book valuable and that you are now equipped with the tools and knowledge to lead your teams effectively. Best of luck in your leadership journey!

References

- Blanchard, K. H., & Johnson, S. (1982). *The One Minute Manager*. William Morrow and Co.
- Daft, R. L. (2017). *The Leadership Experience*. Cengage Learning.
- Garvin, D. A., Edmondson, A. C., & Gino, F. (2008). *Is Yours a Learning Organization?*. Harvard Business Review.
- Hackman, J. R., & Johnson, C. E. (2018). *Leadership: A Communication Perspective*. Waveland Press.
- Hersey, P., & Blanchard, K. H. (1977). *Management of Organizational Behavior: Utilizing Human Resources*. Prentice Hall.
- Kaplan, R. S., & Norton, D. P. (1996). *The Balanced Scorecard: Translating Strategy into Action*. Harvard Business School Press.
- Northouse, P. G. (2019). *Leadership: Theory and Practice*. Sage Publications.

- Rock, D., & Schwartz, J. (2006). *The Neuroscience of Leadership*. Strategy+Business.
- Rogers, E. M. (2003). *Diffusion of Innovations* (5th ed.). Free Press.
- Senge, P. M. (2006). *The Fifth Discipline: The Art & Practice of The Learning Organization*. Doubleday.
- Tannenbaum, R., Weschler, I. R., & Massarik, F. (1961). *Leadership and Organization: A Behavioral Science Approach*. McGraw-Hill.
- Yukl, G. (2013). *Leadership in Organizations*. Pearson.

9 781920 082109